World Series Champions: Atlanta Braves

First baseman Freddie Freeman

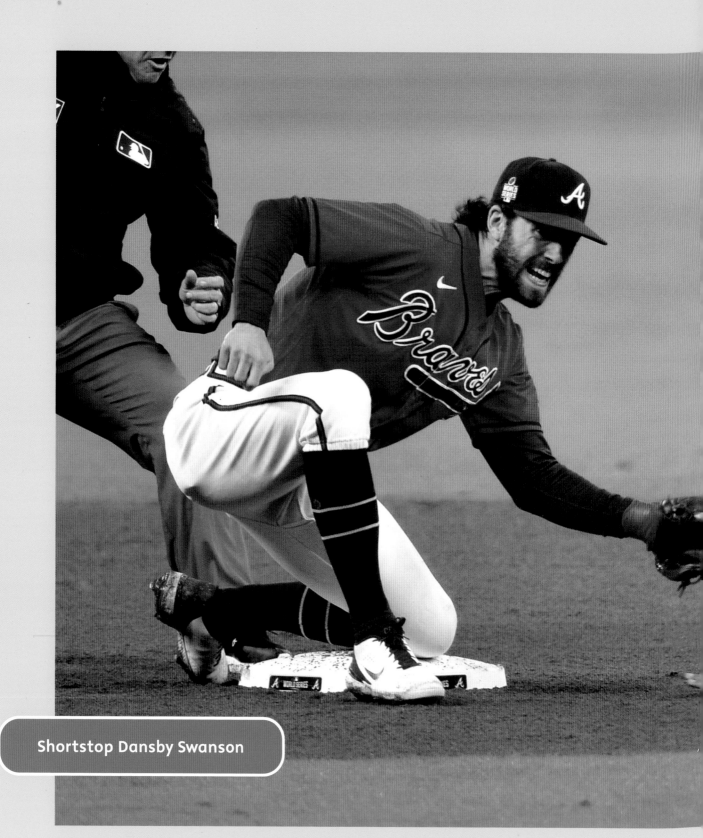

Shortstop Dansby Swanson

WORLD SERIES CHAMPIONS

ATLANTA BRAVES

MICHAEL E. GOODMAN

CREATIVE SPORTS

CREATIVE EDUCATION / CREATIVE PAPERBACKS

Published by Creative Education and Creative Paperbacks
P.O. Box 227, Mankato, Minnesota 56002
Creative Education and Creative Paperbacks are imprints of
The Creative Company
www.thecreativecompany.us

Art Direction by Tom Morgan
Book production by Ciara Beitlich
Edited by Joe Tischler

Photographs by Alamy (ZUMA Press, Inc.), AP Images
(Nick Wass), Getty (Kevin C. Cox, Monica M Davey, Icon
Sportswire, Bob Levey, Hy Peskin Archive, Rich Pilling,
Robert Riger, Edward M Pio Roda, Louis Requena, Daniel
Shirey, George Silk), Shutterstock (Sean Pavone), Wikimedia
Commons (George Kendall Warren)

Library of Congress Cataloging-in-Publication Data
Names: Goodman, Michael E., author.
Title: Atlanta Braves / Michael E. Goodman.
Description: Mankato : Creative Education and Creative
    Paperbacks, [2024] | Series: Creative sports: World Series
    champions | Includes index. | Audience: Ages 7-10 |
    Audience: Grades 2-3 | Summary: "Elementary-level text
    and engaging sports photos highlight the Atlanta Braves'
    MLB World Series wins and losses, plus sensational players
    associated with the professional baseball team such as
    Freddie Freeman."-- Provided by publisher.
Identifiers: LCCN 2023008216 (print) | LCCN 2023008217
    (ebook) | ISBN 9781640268159 (library binding) | ISBN
    9781682773659 (paperback) | ISBN 9781640009851 (pdf)
Subjects: LCSH: Atlanta Braves (Baseball team)--History-
    -Juvenile literature. | Baseball players--United States--
    Juvenile literature.
Classification: LCC GV875.A8 G65 2024 (print) | LCC GV875.A8
    (ebook) | DDC 796.357/6409758231--dc23/eng/20230222
LC record available at https://lccn.loc.gov/2023008216
LC ebook record available at https://lccn.loc.gov/2023008217

Printed in China

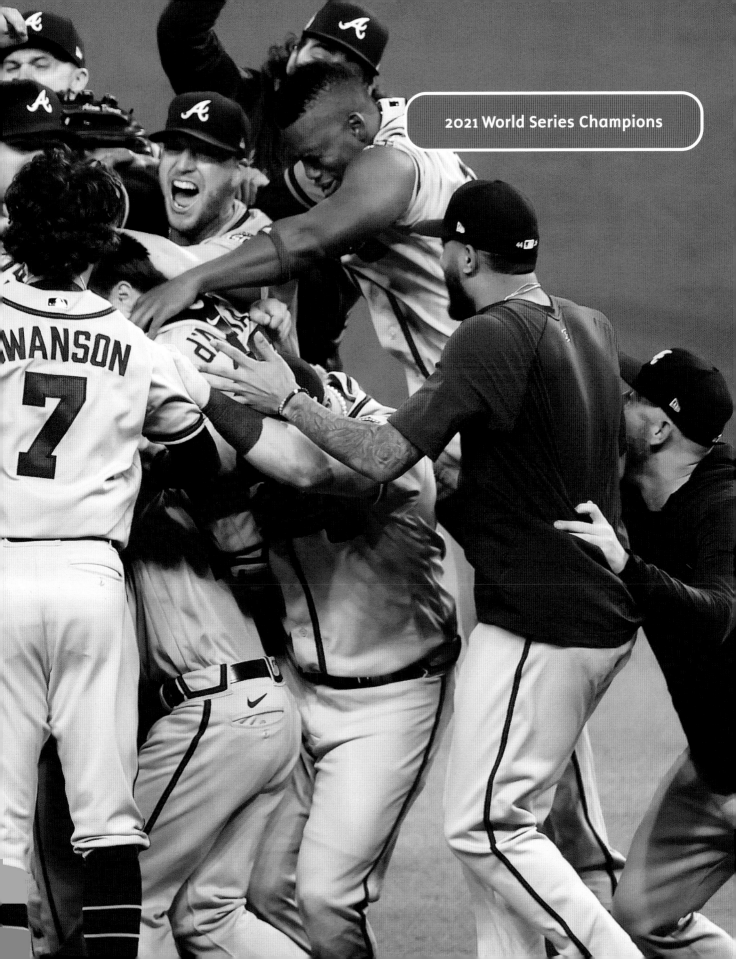

2021 World Series Champions

Third baseman Eddie Mathews

CONTENTS

Home of the Braves

Atlanta, Georgia, is a city on the move. It has the busiest airport in the world. It also has fast-moving trains and lots of cars. Many of those cars carry baseball fans to a **stadium** called Truist Park. The Braves baseball team plays there.

The Atlanta Braves are a Major League Baseball (MLB) team. They play in the National League (NL) East Division. One of their biggest **rivals** are the New York Mets. All MLB teams try to win the World Series to become champions. The Braves have won four World Series **titles**.

George Wright, Boston Red Stockings

Naming the Braves

he team began playing in Boston, Massachusetts, in 1871. They were called the Red Stockings. They had many other nicknames, too. Among them were Beaneaters and Doves. Finally, in 1912, they became the Braves. The team owner belonged to a political group that called its members "Braves."

Pitcher Lew Burdette

Braves History

Boston won eight NL pennants before 1900. Many losing seasons followed. Then in 1914, the Braves jumped from last place to first. They won four straight World Series games. They were champions for the first time! Fans called them the "Miracle Braves."

In 1953, the Braves moved to Milwaukee, Wisconsin. Four years later, they won their second World Series. Pitcher Lew Burdette tossed every inning for three games. He and his team beat the powerful New York Yankees.

In 1966, the team moved south to Atlanta. Third baseman Eddie Mathews hit over 500 career home runs. Outfielder Hank Aaron did even better. "Hammerin' Hank" set a then-major league record. He smashed 755 homers.

ATLANTA BRAVES

Pitcher Greg Maddux

In 1995, **Hall of Fame** pitcher Greg Maddux led the Braves to their third World Series title. Two of his pitching teammates—John Smoltz and Tom Glavine—are also in the Hall of Fame. So is switch-hitting third baseman Chipper Jones.

The Braves won a fourth World Series in 2021. Slugging first baseman Freddie Freeman was a special star. So was hard-hitting shortstop Dansby Swanson.

Other Braves Stars

tlanta fans have cheered for many outstanding pitchers. Two favorites were knuckleball specialist Phil Niekro and hard-throwing lefty Warren Spahn. Both won more than 300 games in their careers.

Manager Bobby Cox guided the Braves to 15 **playoff** appearances. He pushed his players to do their best.

Pitcher Warren Spahn

Outfielder Ronald Acuña Jr.

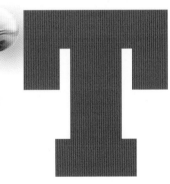

Today, Atlanta is counting on speedy slugger Ronald Acuña Jr. and flame-throwing pitcher Kyle Wright. Fans hope they can bring another championship to Truist Park soon.

About the Braves

Started playing: 1871

· ·

League/division: National
    League, East Division

· ·

Team colors: navy blue, red, and white

· ·

Home stadium: Truist Park

· ·

WORLD SERIES CHAMPIONSHIPS:

   1914, 4 games to 0 over
   Philadelphia Athletics

· ·

   1957, 4 games to 3 over
   New York Yankees

· ·

   1995, 4 games to 2 over
   Cleveland Indians

· ·

   2021, 4 games to 2 over
   Houston Astros

· ·

Atlanta Braves website:
   www.mlb.com/braves

· ·

Glossary

Hall of Fame—a museum in which the best players of all time are honored

....

pennant—a league championship; a team that wins a pennant gets to play in the World Series

....

playoffs—games that the best teams play after a regular season to see who the champion will be

....

rival—a team that plays extra hard against another team

....

stadium—a building with tiers of seats for spectators

....

title—another word for championship

....

WORLD SERIES CHAMPIONS

Pitcher Kyle Wright

Index